BREVE HISTORIA SOBRE EL TITANIC

Datos históricos fascinantes sobre la tragedia del Titanic

SCOTT MATTHEWS

Relics of a Hidden Paradise

Deep in the woods, where the sunlight won't go,
Lies a bloom that forgot how to glow.
It tried sprouting colors, but all that it wore,
Were shades of embarrassment, nothing more.

With roots tangled up in a dance of despair,
It called out to critters, 'Do you even care?'
They laughed and they flitted, a code in their tune,
Very smart for a flower, but alas! Not a boon.

The Last Whispers of the Lilies

Once stood a cluster of proud, flouncy blooms,
They'd gossip and giggle, spreading their fumes.
But today, they whispered in a tone quite absurd,
'Is anyone here? Or are we just blurred?'

They pondered their fragrance, a faint little tease,
'Sometimes being delightful is such a disease!
Perhaps it's the potting, or maybe the sun,
When brought to the market, will we be outdone?'

A Melody of Radiant Absence

In the corner of gardens, where shadows are cast,
Resides a shy bloom, wishing to last.
Though its petals are shy and its stem a frail thing,
It dreams of the day it can finally sing.

With a dance of the wind, it gives quite a show,
But the audience laughs, 'Is it ever a pro?'
Chasing a breeze, it leaps and it sways,
Yet nobody notices, lost in the craze!

Unwritten Verses of the Garden

In a patch where weeds embrace,
A lone flower dreams of space.
She thinks of grandeur, tall and bright,
But trips on roots, oh what a sight!

Once she swayed with all her friends,
Now the sunlight just pretends.
Butterflies dance, but they don't see,
Her antics make the bees all flee!

Rainclouds come and drop their tears,
She tells them jokes to cheer their fears.
With every droplet, laughter glows,
Her petals blush, they steal the show!

So here she stands, with crooked grin,
A crown of daisies on her chin.
Though overlooked, she thrives in fun,
A comic queen—her reign's begun!

Blooms in the Land of Shadows

In a corner where shadows creep,
There's a bloom that's lost its leap.
With wilted dreams she tries to thrive,
A wannabe star, just not alive!

A squirrel once claimed her for a seat,
Giggling at her lack of heat.
She threw a leaf, said, "Take your trot!"
But he just laughed, oh what a plot!

The moonlight's bright, but she feels none,
Her petals whisper, longing fun.
A gnome nearby gives her a wink,
"Join the party! Don't you think?"

So in her mind, she starts to dance,
In a world where she takes a chance.
With every giggle, she breaks the mold,
A tale of charm, forever told!

A Reverie of the Neglected Blossom

Once there bloomed a flower shy,
In a garden where few pass by.
She plotted schemes to catch their eyes,
But ended up with silly pies!

Her petals frill, they twist and twine,
In the breeze, she tries to shine.
But insects giggle at her style,
"Are you blooming or just in denial?"

Amidst the grass, she starts a show,
With puns and jokes, her secrets flow.
A thistle heckles loud and clear,
But she just turns, "My dear, oh dear!"

Embracing shade, she finds delight,
In all the follies of her plight.
Though shunned by many, she still beams,
A jester's heart in floral dreams!

Botanicals in the Shadows

In a garden where plants wear hats,
Wearing blooms that hold the chats.
They gossip about the sun's bright beams,
While orchids nap in their own dreams.

Sneaky vines wrap around a chair,
Throwing shade like they just don't care.
With petals lost in a dance of grace,
They chuckle softly, their secret place.

A Chorus of Unseen Blooms

A flower band plays for folks who pass,
But the trumpet's missing—oh what a sass!
Petals sway to a tune so sweet,
Yet, they all trip on their own two feet.

They sing of rain and sunlit cheer,
While bees buzz by but won't come near.
A melody lost in a leafy grove,
The audience nods, but few will strove.

Portraits of Dappled Light

In sunlight's play, shadows make them grin,
With bragging rights, they draw you in.
Their petals glow in a quirky spot,
While one claims fame for being forgot.

A painter's brush tries to capture this,
But it laughs back with a petal kiss.
Colorful mischief, a hilarious sight,
Creating laughter from morning till night.

The Lost Language of Petals

Once, petals knew all the languages,
With dialects of scents and funny phrases.
They organized a meeting in the dark,
But forgot who'd come—it missed the spark!

They whispered tales of days gone by,
While collecting dust, oh my, oh my!
With laughter echoing through the air,
Their secrets linger but few will care.

A Palette of Disregarded Beauty

In a garden tucked away, so shy,
A bloom just sneezed, oh my, oh my!
Velvet petals, dusty and rare,
Whispering secrets they'd like to share.

Gnomes and fairies play hide and seek,
While color fades, it's quite the peak!
With a giggle, they shimmy and sway,
While bees buzz lazily, on their way.

A ladybug winks, 'Hey, look at me!'
"Never mind the weeds, I'm fancy-free!"
The sun dips low, a glorious sight,
A dance of chaos, all feels just right.

Echoes of a Garden's Heart

In the shade where shadows prance,
Petals gather for their dance.
Whispers of laughter, a riotous crew,
Echoing memories of morning dew.

Sunflowers giggle, "Aren't we tall?"
While daisies mumble, "You're not that small!"
In this wild chaos, a frog jumps high,
Croaking out jokes as the dragonflies fly.

Amongst the roses, a bumblebee grins,
"Your scent is lovely, but my humor wins!"
Tickled by breezes, the leaves start to sway,
In a garden where jokes grow each day.

Stolen Moments Among the Flora

Between the blooms, a squirrel has fun,
Stashing acorns like treasure, oh what a run!
A daisy shouts, "You're a real thief!"
He laughs with a twitch, "Just a little mischief!"

Petunias gossip, "Did you hear the news?"
That tulip thinks it can wear fancy shoes!
In a world of petals and leafy charades,
The critters all join in the playful parades.

Under the gaze of the moonlight's beam,
A hedgehog sports a whimsical dream.
Laughter erupts from a little bluebird,
As secrets are shared, rarely unheard.

The Remnants of Hidden Splendor

In a corner, an ancient vine lies,
With a toothy grin and mischievous eyes.
"Remember me?" it chuckles in glee,
As the petals twirl and dance with glee.

Tangled stories of flowers past,
Comedic tales in a wild cast.
The lilies prance while the daisies roll,
Joking about who takes the cake bowl.

A sleepy old garden, rich with jest,
Where every bloom believes it's the best.
In the twilight, the petals conspire,
To craft a legend, one that inspires.

The Abandoned Sanctuary

In the garden where dust bunnies play,
The petals lie still, in disarray.
A gnome holds a sign that reads, 'Beware!'
While squirrels chuckle, they comb their hair.

A bench creaks, holding tales untold,
Of fairies who danced with wings of gold.
But now the weeds throw a grand parade,
As crickets sing tunes from long-faded balades.

The fountain sputters with grumpy delight,
While vines, like snickers, climb up in spite.
An owl pretends to read a book,
As I share my thoughts—who'll take a look?

In this forgotten nook, life spins a yarn,
Where laughter takes root in every barn.
Though nature's gone wild and out of tune,
I've made a new friend—a giggling raccoon!

Unseen Wonders of the Wilderness

Among the ferns, a creature lurks,
With floppy ears and curious quirks.
It claims to be a mighty sage,
Yet hides behind a leafy page.

A snail slides by, quite late for a race,
Declaring with pride it won first place.
The trees chuckle, their branches sway,
As shadows dance in a goofy ballet.

A lone butterfly lands on my nose,
Tickling my senses, how funny it goes!
While the river whispers old jokes from the past,
I giggle along, oh, this fun cannot last!

In this odd realm where mischief thrives,
Every critter in sight has its way of jives.
For beauty's not just in blooms, we'll see,
It's also in laughter, wild and free!

Echoes in Twilight Hues

As the sun dips low, the shadows dance,
A party of critters, not leaving to chance.
The twilight hums with giggles and squeaks,
While fireflies glitter—it's fun that peaks!

A raccoon, a fox, and a wise old crow,
Tell tales of the day, and oh how they flow!
Each story a mix of truth and jest,
While the moon winks down, all snug in her nest.

The backdrop glows in splendid grins,
As night's velvet cloak wraps around the skins.
A chameleon claims it's the queen of disguise,
In polka dots, it slinks, to our wild surprise.

In this serenade, where the giggles grow,
Even the shadows join in the show.
For every whisper in evening's arms,
Echoes the fun of nature's charms!

The Lullaby of Hidden Blooms

In a corner of chaos, blooms start to snore,
While a bear in pajamas snoozes on the floor.
The daisies whisper secrets, while giggling tight,
At dreams of wild nights under moon's soft light.

While frogs toss and turn in their lily pad beds,
The stars roll their eyes, laughing at threads.
They play peek-a-boo through the tall grass maze,
While the flowers awake in a colorful daze.

A spider spins tales with silken finesse,
Of mischief and laughter, it's quite a mess!
As night turns to laughter, embracing its tune,
Forgetfulness reigns, as mischief's a boon.

So here in this hue, where the whimsy is found,
A lullaby lingers, soft, safe, and sound.
For the blooms and the critters in slumber's embrace,
Forever shall cradle this joyous space!

A Garden's Silent Cry

In a corner, all alone,
Sits a plant, a little prone.
Its petals wear a dusting gray,
Wishing for a brighter day.

Bugs pass by without a glance,
Dancing flowers steal the chance.
In silence, it begins to pout,
Wondering what it's all about.

A gnome shakes his tiny fist,
"You're blooming! Don't you get the gist?"
But the lonely orchid sighs,
"Do they see me? That's the prize!"

Shadows of a Fading Petal

In the dark, it quietly waits,
Behind the roses, near the gates.
It dreams of colors, nice and bright,
While others bask in sheer delight.

A squirrel winks, then scurries by,
Whispering softly, "Don't be shy!"
But the flower just rolls its eyes,
"You're all just pawns in nature's lies!"

Once a star, now a side show,
It grumbles low, but won't let go.
With every breeze, it flops and sways,
Protesting in peculiar ways!

Echoing Sighs of Nature

In a jungle of bright cheer,
Here sits a petal, quite austere.
With a frown that would stop clocks,
It wonders where all the fun talks!

A parrot squawks, "You wear that well!"
The bloom just quips, "Oh, do tell!"
"Can't you add some vibrant hue?
All I see is grey and blue!"

Every butterfly troubles near,
But only to sneak a little sneer.
"Who knew flowers had such sass?
If you bloom, they'll all come past!"

Blooms that Time Forgot

In a pot that nobody chose,
Lives a plant nobody knows.
Each morning, it whispers loud,
"Why can't I join the flower crowd?"

A dandelion laughs, "Oh please,
Your shade gives gardens such unease!"
But the flower just gives a grin,
"Watch me sparkle, let's begin!"

As days pass without a change,
Does it feel wild or just strange?
'Cause when it blooms, the world may see,
Even oddballs can be fancy!

Lingering Aromas of Yesteryear

In a garden where dreams once danced,
Lies a flower with a mischievous stance.
It sneezes pollen when you draw near,
Causing all nearby folks to cheer.

The bees can't find where to play,
"Is that perfume, or yesterday's buffet?"
With petals that giggle in the sun,
Even the ants think it's all in fun.

The gardener laughs with a wink and a nod,
As the blooms gossip like a modern squad.
"Did you hear what happened to the old bay?
They tried to prune, but he went astray!"

So here it fades, in a flair of jest,
This flower of life that never takes rest.
With aromas that tickle and memories that tease,
It lingers on, just to please the bees.

The Lost Symphony of Petals

Once in a meadow, a handful of blooms,
Played symphonies while the daylight looms.
With trumpet vines and dainty tunes,
They got the squirrels tapping their shoes!

A rose quipped, "This is quite the show!"
But tulips responded, "Oh, please, take it slow!"
The daisies chimed in, "We've got needs,"
"More like a concert of wild weeds!"

A thunderstorm hit, and away they ran,
Each petal scouting for the best hiding plan.
"When the music starts, we'll bring back the fun,"
Yelled the orchids, dreaming of the sun.

Yet when the skies clear, they laugh and play,
Those blossoms rejoicing in the light of day.
For hidden melodies in the breeze,
Make even the sunflowers bob with ease.

A Solitary Bloom's Tale

In a corner of the yard, all alone,
Blooms a flower with a curious tone.
It thinks to itself, "What fun can I seek?"
While waiting for friends, it's turned quite meek.

"Maybe I'll dance with the old garden hose,
Or throw a soirée for the nearby crows."
But every wild idea, it thinks twice on,
"Just me and this soil, how fun can that be, hon?"

Then one fine day, the sun shines bright,
A bee buzzes in, bringing pure delight.
"Come join my party, it's a real hoot!"
Together they sway, oh, what a hoot!

From lonely to lively, the bloom takes a chance,
With laughter and joy, it begins to prance.
For even a flower, all by itself,
Can throw the best bash upon the shelf!

Beneath the Weight of Time

In a pot so dusty, wisdom amassed,
A flower ponders its forgotten past.
"Once I was vibrant, oh so bold,
Now I'm just stories, rarely retold."

It dreams of the days when it caught the eye,
Of butterflies dancing in a bright July.
"Now my petals sag, my color's off chart,
Yet I still sport this great, flaring heart!"

With a sprinkle of rain and a dash of sun,
It plots a comeback, it's time for some fun!
"I'll bloom with laughter, I shan't be denied,
Who cares if my leaves have lost their pride?"

So down it leans, to give time a twist,
With every new day, it fights to persist.
For in the grand tale of flowers and grime,
Even the tired can fuse joy with time.

Fluttering Memories of a Forsaken Garden

In a garden lost, a tale is spun.
Flowers whisper secrets, oh what fun!
A bee wearing glasses, quite the sight,
Tripped on a petal, oh what a fright!

The roses rolled their eyes, so sly,
While daisies giggled as they passed by.
Sunshine tickled the weeds standing tall,
All joined the party, having a ball!

But wait, there's a plant with quite the pout,
A silly little sprout, full of doubt.
Wishing for laughter, a friend or two,
To dance with the crickets, join in the cue.

So if you wander where laughter blooms,
Look for the giggles in forgotten rooms.
For even the silence has tales to share,
In a place where flowers have naught a care!

Fragrance of Vanished Dreams

In a breeze, a scent from days gone by,
Tickling noses as it flutters by.
The lilacs chuckle, the daisies sway,
They share inside jokes in their own way!

A bumblebee buzzes with a grin,
Sipping nectar, then retrying again.
"Oops, pardon me!" he jovially quips,
As he lands on a petal, taking a dip.

The moonflowers whisper at twilight's call,
Swapping gossip in the garden hall.
From lost blooms, a fragrance escapes,
Tickling the dreams of the soil's capes.

Yet in the shadows, a joke's enshrined,
A wilted weed with a smirk so blind.
"Life's quite a puzzle, my leafy friend,
But let's laugh together till the very end!"

The Tale of the Shadowed Flower

In a corner dark, where sunlight scarce,
Grew a flower shy, with quite the hair,
It wore a hat made of garden weeds,
Spouting wisecracks, planting laughs like seeds.

In the moon's glow, it shimmied and danced,
Making moonbeams giggle as it pranced.
"Oh, look at me! I'm quite the star!"
But nobody noticed—par for the course, bizarre!

A squirrel nearby tried to join the fun,
But tripped on a root, oh what a run!
"I was just practicing my acorn toss,"
He chuckled while tangled, feeling like a boss!

But wisdom eludes the one in shade,
For joy grows brighter when not afraid.
Though at times overlooked, flowers bloom,
With laughter to chase away the gloom!

Sheltered in Nature's Embrace

Amidst the ferns where the shadows play,
A cluster of petals found their way.
They whispered secrets to ants on parade,
"Life's a wild dance, not meant to fade!"

A butterfly flutters, wearing a tie,
With polka dots and colors that electrify.
He jokes with the flowers, "I'm here for the show,
Let's twirl in the wind; let the laughter flow!"

The sun peeked in with a twinkling eye,
Dodging the clouds just passing by.
"Don't leave me out!" chirped a curious seed,
"Join the ruckus, and let's all take heed!"

So in nature's snug, a party unfolds,
With petals and wings, the laughter molds.
For in hidden places, where whispers embrace,
Joy grows like wildflowers, a laugh in every space!

Eclipsed by Time's Passing

In a garden where laughter fades,
An old bloom thinks it's got it made.
With petals stuck in a gossip spree,
It spills secrets on a buzzing bee.

Once bright and bold, now rather shy,
It dons a hat made of crumpled pie.
Waving at weeds with dainty flair,
But no one notices, oh, despair!

A joke to the sun, a riddle to rain,
Telling tales of its long-lost fame.
Yet in the dusk, it steals the show,
With exaggerated tales of woe!

Petals askew, it strikes a pose,
"Look at me! I'm the star, I suppose!"
The critters chuckle, the shadows dance,
As the once-mighty bloom takes a silly stance.

Dreams Lost Amongst the Leaves

A sprout once dreamed of becoming grand,
But found itself stuck in a boggy land.
It whispers to leaves, "Oh, what's my fate?"
But all they do is giggle and wait!

"Rise up," they tease, "or stay where you are,
There's a snail with dreams of being a star!"
The droopy petals start to sway,
As wind tickles tales of a glorious day.

Chasing sunshine with a wobbly twist,
Imagining parties no one would miss.
But the trees just snicker, and the squirrels applaud,
While our sprout contemplates, "Should I be odd?"

In a whirlwind of laughter, it gives a sigh,
"Who needs heights when you can fly high?"
And dreams on the ground are quite the delight,
In a garden where whimsy blooms bright.

Shadows in the Ferns

Beneath the ferns where shadows greet,
A flower sighs, "I hear defeat!"
It tries to pout, yet giggles so loud,
As fireflies gather and form a crowd.

"Where's the spotlight, where's my fame?"
It shimmies around, "Oh, what a game!"
The ferns just rustle, "Whatever, dear!"
As they hum a tune that only they hear.

With every twist, it strikes a pose,
While critters declare, "Hey, look at those!"
They point and jest, "Is that what you call,
A bloom so shy it's scared of it all?"

Yet beneath the laughter, a truth does bloom,
In shadows, true joy finds plenty of room.
So who needs a stage, or spotlights that burn,
When giggles and warmth are what you can earn?

The Solitary Bloom's Farewell

In a lonely plot where daisies joke,
One bloom stirs, as if it awoke.
"Is it time for a trip?" it ponders with glee,
But the daisies quip, "You're stuck like a flea!"

"Don't forget your hat, and never your grin,
As you head out to twirl on a whim!"
A leaf whispers softly, "I'll miss you a lot,
But don't go getting all fancy and caught!"

With petals prepared, it lifts up high,
But tumbles down like a clumsy pie.
The daisies roar, "Oh, what a sight!
Trying to believe you can take flight!"

So off it sets, with a wink and a swirl,
"Look at me, world, I'm a fabulous girl!"
Yet lands with a plop in a nearby stew,
And the daisies cackle, "We always knew!

Serenity in Forgotten Spaces

In a garden where weeds dance,
An old shoe finds romance.
With gnomes that play peek-a-boo,
And a cat that thinks it's a kangaroo.

Mossy stones wear a crown,
While squirrels steal the show with a frown.
The daisies giggle, oh so bright,
Chasing shadows in the fading light.

The compost heap has tales to tell,
Of worms that dream, oh so well.
A trowel rests with a sigh of glee,
As bumblebees sip herbal tea.

In corners where the sun forgot,
A rubber duck can be their plot.
Each bloom that pops with a joyful cheer,
Hums a tune for all to hear.

The Essence of Whispering Blooms

A daffodil tells a corny joke,
While tulips giggle till they choke.
Lilies wear their hats askew,
Spilling secrets, just a few.

A rose blushes, gossip in tow,
"Did you hear what the violets know?"
Butterflies float with perfect grace,
Buzzing laughter fills the space.

Dandelions blow their fluffy wishes,
While snickers rise from muddy dishes.
Sunflowers dance in the gentle breeze,
Telling the moon, "Say cheese, please!"

The bees, oh what a busy crew,
Write floral scripts, the whole day through.
In the chaos, there's a funny twist,
As petals whisper, it can't be missed.

Timeworn Treasures Amongst the Green

In the garden lies a rusty fork,
Claiming it once danced with a stork.
Old boots hold a secret tale,
Of adventures where cucumbers sail.

A pot cracked wide, a home for snails,
While ivy tells ghost stories of trails.
Worn-out chairs where fairies sit,
To laugh at the world, just a bit.

Leaves scribble notes in a playful flight,
As hedgehogs argue about the night.
Tangled vines wrap around the past,
Whispering secrets that hold fast.

Each stone a witness to laughter shared,
Under the sun, all worries bared.
Timeworn treasures in every hue,
Creating joy in the morning dew.

The Boughs that Hold No Secrets

Branches sway in the breezy play,
Chasing squirrels who've gone astray.
With acorns laughing from on high,
While chipmunks practice their spy-sigh.

The leaves conspire with the gentle breeze,
To tickle the branches and annoy the trees.
Boughs creak with tales of laughter bold,
As shadows pirouette, a sight to behold.

Underneath, the grass grows wild,
As dandelions dance, nature's child.
Each petal prances, no care at all,
In this whimsical world, they stand tall.

And if you listen, laughter's the tune,
As whispers unravel 'neath the moon.
For in the trees, no secrets bind,
Just giggles echoing in the mind.

Chronicles of the Unnoticed

In a garden tucked away from sight,
A bud that thinks it's quite the fright.
It practices blooms in the dead of night,
While snoozing bees all snore with delight.

A flower swings, the petals sway,
But no one cares, they're all away.
It tells jokes to a passing stray,
Whose tail wags like it's here to stay.

With whispers soft, the leaves do jest,
"Why do you bloom when not a guest?"
The flower sighs, "I've passed the test,
In solitude, I feel quite blessed."

So here it stands in silent cheer,
A secret bloom, no one draws near.
Its petals laugh, "Well, isn't it clear?
I bloom for me, so there's no fear!"

Nature's Unwritten Elegy

In corners where the sunlight creeps,
A flower weeps that no one peeps.
It sings a song, but no one keeps,
The lyrics lost in tangled heaps.

With roots so deep, it shakes with glee,
"There's no audience, just me, just me!"
A snail rolls by, says, "Oh, looky,
You're the star of this greenery!"

It stretches tall, a sight so bold,
Unnoticed stories left untold.
"Why fret?" it grins, "I'm never cold,
My humor's fresh, my rhymes of gold!"

Thus nature hums a tune forlorn,
A band of one on a lazy morn.
Yet every flower, even so worn,
Will crack a smile in its own form.

A Dance with Dust and Memories

In a dusty pot on a windowsill,
An orchid dreams of a grand thrill.
It dances slow, it spins, it will,
But all that's there is a silent chill.

"Hey there, dust mite, come and sway!
You've got the moves that brighten my day."
The dust replied, "I'm on a holiday,
But I can jitter, just for play!"

The sunlight beams, it calls in vain,
"Remember me? I'm bright again!"
But the flower jokes, "Oh, what a pain,
These shadows thrive, they're such a gain!"

So off they twirl, in whimsical leaps,
Amidst the whispers, laughter peeps.
For even lonely, joy still creeps,
In memory's dance, the silence sleeps.

Beneath the Canopy of Forgetting

Beneath the trees where no one goes,
An unseen bloom wears worn-out prose.
It dreams of laughter, tickled toes,
But only moss knows how it glows.

With every breeze, it starts to giggle,
"Life's a party, wait for the wiggle!"
A squirrel chirps, "Hey, don't be fickle,
Your leaves are green, now that's a riddle!"

In the shade, the whispers fly,
"Look at me soar, oh, my! my! my!"
But passing bugs just wave goodbye,
Still, it blooms bright, reaching for the sky.

And so it stands, a joke well-kept,
In shadows where the sun's inept.
It laughs aloud, though all has slept,
"For those who wander, what a jest!"

Entwined in Dust and Memory

In the attic where the shadows play,
A flower pot forgot, in disarray.
Dust bunnies dance, they groove and sway,
While visions of petals dream away.

A gardener's trowel, lost in a fog,
Meets a gnome who's wedged in a bog.
Together they plot a revival scheme,
To bring back life to this withered dream.

The sunlight filtered through cobwebs thin,
Where laughter once thrived, now it's just sin.
Forgotten blooms start to giggle and tease,
With a breeze that jiggles the old, dead leaves.

Oh, the tales this old pot could tell,
Of love and neglect in a floral shell.
A memory dressed in dust's tight embrace,
With a wink from a gnome who's lost in space.

Blooms Lost to the Wind

Once a bloom, now a tumbleweed,
Chasing the breeze like a comedic steed.
Whispers of petals float through the air,
In a slapstick dance, without a care.

Nearby, a squirrel with a nutty grin,
Tries to catch blooms by the tip of its chin.
One sneezes loudly, oh, what a sight,
As flowers burst forth in a floral fight.

Petals pirouette on a gusty day,
Landing on windows, they giggle and sway.
A flower in slippers, oh, what a scene,
Dancing alone, like a prince with no queen.

While bees roll their eyes and buzz up a storm,
Thinking of pollen, their usual norm.
Blooms might be lost, but they giggle and blend,
In the wind's wild laughter, they never quite end.

Timeless Echoes in the Thicket

In the thicket grows laughter, lost in the shade,
Echoes dancing in a floral parade.
A daisy declares it's a joke-telling king,
While vines twine around like a slapstick fling.

A rabbit hops in with a top hat on tight,
Reciting old riddles, what a silly sight.
Nearby, a thrush joins in with a song,
Warning the flowers, 'You won't last long!'

Bumbles and giggles, nature's jesters gather,
A wallflower blushing, oh, what a clatter!
Jokes played on petals with a humorous crack,
Timeless echoes humorously flap and stack.

The thicket's a stage; let the laughter unfold,
Where stories of blooms and antics are told.
Though once lush and proud, they now fumble and bide,
In the hallowed thicket, they bloom alongside.

Fragrance of Yesterday's Dreams

A whiff of perfume from a garden long gone,
Sprinkled with chuckles from dusk until dawn.
The flowers reminisce of their vibrant past,
With giggles and scents, their memories cast.

A peony pranks the dull rocks by the stream,
With petals so vivid, they shine and they gleam.
"Remember the bees?" the lilac chimes in,
"Who danced on our heads with a cheeky grin?"

Petals nap under soft whispers of night,
While dreams flutter past like a whimsical kite.
"Let's throw a party!" the poppy suggests,
While the daisies snicker, "Keep dreaming, don't rest!"

Yet fragrances linger, a soft memory game,
With laughter and whimsy, none feel any shame.
Though time may erase, and flowers may fade,
In the scent of yesterday, joy is displayed.

The Abandoned Sanctuary of Scent

In a garden once lush, now twisted and bare,
Stands an old flower pot, missing its pair.
It dreams of the sunshine, yet hangs in regret,
Recalling the moments it once had a pet.

A butterfly chuckles, its wings full of glee,
Dancing around weeds that grow wild and free.
The pot starts to wonder, 'Where did I go wrong?'
Maybe it's time to join the dance, sing along!

The petals are absent, the soil is so dry,
Yet jokingly plans another grand sky-high.
A dandelion giggles, declares it the king,
Waving its fluff like a silly old thing.

But in this odd place where laughter feels right,
Even ghosts of old blooms find joy in the night.
And though love was once lost, with humor they cope,
Making merry where sadness once lost all hope.

Ghosts in the Greenhouse

In a greenhouse bustling with shadows and fright,
Lurking among plants, those ghosts take to flight.
They whisper of petals long faded away,
Now a poltergeist orchid in need of a play.

"Boo!" said the fern, with a shiver and shake,
"I miss the sunbathing, for goodness' sake!"
The swag of the cactus, with spines like a joke,
Adds to the laughter, each time that it spoke.

A rose rolls its eyes, with a sigh of despair,
"I once stole the show, now no one will care."
But the ivy insists, "With a twist and a bend,
We'll host a wild party, where we all can pretend!"

So the ghosts all gathered, with charm in the air,
Clinking their petals in a whimsical chair.
Lost among memories, they danced through the gloom,
Just a playful reminder that flowers can bloom.

Lament of a Forsaken Flower

A petal that droops, with a twinge in its heart,
Once bright and the star, now an oil painting's part.
It sighs to the breeze, "Where did my friends go?"
While a busy bee buzzes, "You've high drama, though!"

The grass all around is a laughing brigade,
Practicing jokes in this sunny charade.
"Have you heard the one about the wilting bloom?"
It's funny, yet sad—the flower felt doomed.

It looked in a mirror, saw its frazzled old self,
Wishing for days when it sat on the shelf.
"Oh, why am I lonely? Where's my vibrant crew?"
A worm crawls on by, saying, "Hey, we all feel blue!"

So, with a deep breath, it dares to stand tall,
"Let's raise a good laugh; let's throw a grand ball!"
With shadows of laughter, they banter and cling,
Making peace with the past as they dance and sing.

Petals of Nostalgia

In a vase full of memories, colors once bright,
A story unfolds in the pale morning light.
This bloom's got tales of romance and glee,
But now it just dreams of the days that used to be.

"Once, I was sprightly!" the petal did boast,
"I twirled with the daisies, a true garden host!"
But a rogue spider laughed, spinning webs of dismay,
"Look at you now, you're just withered and gray!"

"So what!" cried the bloom, with a wink and a grin,
"Let's throw a grand bash, invite all from within!"
So they gathered the weeds, the thorns, and the dust,
Declaring adventure, as all flowers must.

A riot of petals, all laughing in cheer,
Transformed a sad room into heartfelt veneer.
As nostalgia took root, blending joy with a sigh,
They blossomed together, with love reaching high.

Secrets of the Hidden Blossom

In a garden where no one dared to stroll,
Lived a flower with a quirky little soul.
It wore mismatched petals, quite a sight,
Sipping dew under the moon's soft light.

It giggled at bees who forgot their way,
And threw pollen parties at the break of day.
With roots that danced and leaves that twirled,
It whispered secrets to the dreaming world.

One day a snail thought he'd play the spy,
But tripped on a stem and let out a sigh.
The flower just chuckled, what a fine mess,
"Next time, dear snail, wear shoes, I guess!"

So if you wander near the hidden spot,
And hear laughter, give it a shot.
For among the weeds, joy often hides,
In blooms of laughter where nature abides.

Petals Beneath the Dust

In the corner of the yard, a tale unfolds,
Of petals under dust, and stories untold.
A daisy tried hard to become a star,
But settled for a sandwich, oh, how bizarre!

It grumbled at the roses, so prim and so neat,
"Can't you lighten up, I've got crumbs for a treat!"
The lilies rolled eyes, full of disdain,
While the orchids just giggled, rather insane.

Then one sunny day, the dust danced away,
Revealing a show of the green and the gray.
"Look!" said the daisy, "I'm fancy and bright!"
But the weeds around whispered, "Oh, what a sight!"

So if you ever feel low on the ground,
Remember the dust can turn up the sound.
For under the grime lies a party so bold,
Where laughter and petals are always gold.

A Wilted Dream in Twilight

In a pot on the windowsill, there lived a dream,
Wilted and weary, plotting a scheme.
It wanted to bloom but fell asleep,
While a dancing cactus made fun, oh so deep.

"Hey wilted buddy, don't look so glum!"
Said the cactus with a sway and a bum.
"You just need a party, perhaps a feast,
With good soil and sunshine, be a happy beast!"

The dream yawned wide, and stretched its poor leaves,
"I'd rather just lounge and take what life weaves."
But suddenly a bee brought sweet nectar's call,
And the wilted one chuckled, "Let's have a ball!"

So under the stars, they danced till dawn,
The forgotten dream, now happily drawn.
Sometimes all it takes is a little delight,
To turn a wilted heart into pure, shining light.

The Orchid That Was Never Seen

In a realm where flowers pretend to be grand,
There sat an orchid, oh what a bland brand!
It hid in the shadows, avoiding the sun,
Claiming, "I'm rare, let's just have some fun!"

"Oh look at me!" the dandelions gushed,
While the orchid just giggled, "I'm truly crushed!"
"I'm virtually invisible, do you dare?"
Yet all of them laughed, "We see no flair!"

In the moonlight, it twirled with such grace,
Wishing for petals to take it to space.
But instead it just hung, amidst twirls and twists,
Confident, who cares if it's lost in the mist?

So if you spot blooms that seem a bit shy,
Remember the orchid is too good to lie.
For sometimes the hidden can dance the best tune,
In the garden of life, where dreams can't be pruned.

Haunt of the Pale Flower

In a garden where laughter grows,
Stood a flower with curious prose.
It giggled each time the wind blew,
Whispering secrets, while sipping dew.

Once bright, now a shade of white,
The petals dance in the moonlight.
A ghost of a bloom, it sways with glee,
As bees tease it, 'Just wait and see!'

Around the pot, all critters peek,
A comical show, so silly, so chic.
With every twist, its stalk would bend,
'Watch out!' it cried, 'You might just spend!'

So if you wander to that old patch,
And hear a chuckle mixed with a scratch,
Know it's just that flower, quite absurd,
With witty quips and tales unheard.

Whispers in the Wilted Leaves

Beneath the branches, leaves all fray,
A twisted tale runs wild each day.
The wilted greens, they gossip so,
About the flower, who steals the show.

'Look at that one, its humor's grand!
Always telling jokes, far from bland!
Though fading fast, it reigns supreme,
As laughter echoes, a silly dream.

With petals drooping, it still stands proud,
Claiming space in the bustling crowd.
'Why did the bee sit on my nose?'
It chortled out, everyone knows!

So come and listen to tales long told,
Of that cheeky bloom, not meek, but bold.
In a yard where humor's the ultimate tease,
The wilted flower brings all to their knees!

Fragments of a Past Bloom

Once a regal queen of the glade,
Now a jester in a sunbeam parade.
With petals that giggle and sway just right,
It tells of days that were full of light.

"Oh look at me, the ruler of dirt,
With pollen-capped jokes for a humorous hurt!
What's funnier still, look! I'm quite bare,
Though I used to have many a vibrant hair!"

The garden critters just snicker and roll,
As it pulls up a root to amuse the whole soul.
'Time has turned me a tad on the sly,'
It beams at the sky, 'But hey, I still fly!'

So if you find that old patch of cheer,
Join in the laughter, let go of your fear.
For every droopy petal has a tale to give,
In the left-behind bloom, we still deeply live!

The Ephemeral Dreamscape

In a dream where flowers giggle at night,
A quirky petal glimmers in frosty light.
'Oh, look at my friends, the grass and the weeds!'
Together they dance, on fanciful needs.

'Why grow straight? That's far too plain!
I'll sprout in loops, like a whimsical chain!'
And with a twist and a silly cheer,
Each blossom yells, 'Come join the circus here!'

But the bees just buzz, caught in the thrill,
As this dreamy scene gives their hearts a fill.
With laughter ringing from each rosy hue,
A flowered fairground, where dreams come true.

So next time you nap, beneath the moon's beam,
Remember the garden—a wild, funny dream.
For blooms may fade, but the laughs will remain,
In the echoes of petals, we find joy again!

The Promise of Forgotten Glory

Once bloom was bright, now it's simply shy,
Hiding in shadows, oh my, oh my!
There were whispers of fame, flirtations and glee,
Yet here it stands laughing, so much like me.

A vase once proud, now cramped and small,
Dreams of grandeur become a fall.
If petals could giggle, they'd chuckle with ease,
In the quest for sunshine, they settled for weeds.

So here's to the bloom that once had a flair,
Mixing up colors with not a single care.
It's now a faded echo, a joke in the breeze,
Hiding its laughter among the tall trees.

Forget all the glory, let's just have some fun,
With petals like dreams that won't come undone.
We're all just like blooms, in a pot with a twist,
Chasing our shadows, still raising a fist.

The Enigma of Elusive Petals

In a garden forgotten, a riddle holds tight,
Petals prime for mischief, what a curious sight!
They plot and they scheme, these elusive delights,
Turning from pal to trickster on long summer nights.

Why bloom with pride, when you can be sly?
They tickle the daisies, and giggle on high.
With colors so bright, they tease the front row,
But when you come close, they fake a slow grow.

The nectar's a trap, a sweet sticky joke,
A shenanigan wrapped in a glamour cloak.
They play peek-a-boo underneath shady leaves,
Making all of us believe they're more than thieves.

Oh, mischievous petals, keep laughing in shade,
Your absence brings smiles in the daylight parade.
In the whispers of gardens, your antics will tell,
Of bloopers and blunders where flowers once fell.

A Soliloquy of Withered Leaves

Once born with a flair, now crumpled and mute,
Leaves talking nonsense while standing astute.
They reminisce about sunlight, and rain-drenched days,
While getting a tan in the sun's warm rays.

The grand tale of growth, now a comedy scene,
When they try to dance, it's more like a glean.
In their rusty old coats, with humor so dry,
They reminisce softly, a nostalgic sigh.

Oh, to be young in the prime of the show,
Not crumbling and cracked in a pitiful row.
But laughter is timeless, it dances like air,
In the realm of the withered, joy still lays bare.

So here's to the leaves, whose stories endure,
With chuckles and giggles, let's all be sure.
For even in withering, spirits can thrive,
In the chorus of aging, let's dance and survive.

Ethereal Scents of the Overlooked

Amidst the wild weeds, a scent so absurd,
A whiff of the bygone, so petty, unheard.
With notes of sweet chaos, the air does proclaim,
An aroma of giggles, and sunshine to blame.

Neglected and quirky, an essence to share,
While blossoms in gardens catch everyone's stare.
A whiff and a chuckle—they bloom just for jest,
In the shadows, they frolic, who knew they were blessed?

Come closer, they whisper, and take a small whiff,
With stories like candy, they offer a gift.
The scent of their laughter, like secrets on air,
A reminder to revel in joys unaware.

So here's to the overlooked, the funny and shy,
In gardens forgotten, they teach us to fly.
Through humor and essence, let all spirits lift,
In the fragrant embraces, find life's hidden gift.

Whispers of a Lost Bloom

In a garden where jokes never land,
A flower stood silly, no helping hand.
It waved to the bees, without any care,
They buzzed right past, finding snacks elsewhere.

The petals were tickled by breezes that laughed,
Counting the days since it last had a bath.
It tried to wear shoes, but they weren't its size,
And when it danced, oh, what a surprise!

Its roots told a tale of antics and cheer,
But the weeds rolled their eyes, "You're still hanging here?"
Yet with every sunrise, it found new delight,
In the splashes of color that made spirits bright.

So it sang to the sun, a funny old tune,
Dreaming of dinners with daisy and moon.
With laughter and giggles, it bloomed just the same,
For never on earth, is dullness to blame.

Shadows of a Neglected Petal

In shadows where petals once basked in the sun,
A lonely old flower just wanted some fun.
It tried to impress with a dance so divine,
But only the snails cared to follow the line.

The moon peeked in and couldn't help but grin,
At the clumsy old bud in a wild swirl spin.
It tripped on a root, made a raucous old sound,
Even crickets had to chuckle around.

It sent out invites to bees and to ants,
"Come join me for tea, wear your best pants!"
The crowd showed up late, with hats made of grass,
While the sleepy sunflowers just waved as they passed.

Yet through all the slumber and whimsical trails,
This petals' charm danced despite all the fails.
With a giggle and wink, it flourished and grew,
In a garden of laughter, where joy always flew.

Echoes in the Garden of Time

In the garden's old tales, echoes of glee,
There bloomed a small bud, as bright as could be.
It told the old stories of mischief and fun,
How it once pulled a prank on the curious sun.

The daisies all snickered, "Do tell us once more!
How'd you convince him to dance on the floor?"
With a twinkle and giggle, the memory shared,
Of sunlight and shadows, no worries or cares.

The violets chimed in, "We saw it up close,
That flower's a joker, we'll raise it a toast!"
So they throw a wild party, with petals of cheer,
To celebrate laughter that brightened the year.

In silence of twilight, the whispers grew loud,
Of blooms that once flourished, but never were proud.
Yet the memory lingered, sweet laughter entwined,
In the echoes of time, their friendship defined.

In the Silence of Withering Leaves

As autumn crept in, with silence so grim,
A petal sat grumpy, with no joyful whim.
It pondered the sun and the friends it had known,
But the leaves dropped like jokes, in a monotone.

"Why so blue?" asked a twig, "You used to be loud!
Where's the laughter, the fun, that drew in the crowd?"
With a sigh and a frown, the bloom looked around,
"For I think they forgot me, without a sound."

But a squirrel jumped by, with a chuckle and cheer,
"Don't worry, dear petal, your time's still quite near!
For blooms that feel down, can still cause a ruckus,
So let's gather the others and turn it to fuss!"

With giggles and prancing, petals revived,
For sometimes a grump needs a laugh to survive.
In the silence of waning, silliness grew,
A garden of joy, a whimsical view.

Veils of Misted Fragrance

In the garden where nobody strays,
A flower hides in a curious daze.
Its petals part like secrets untold,
With whispers of laughter through marigold.

A bee buzzes by, asking, "Where's the fun?"
The flower replies, "Not much under the sun!"
With a wink and a nod, it ponders the fate,
Of the squirrels laughing at its own awkward gait.

"I'm the belle of the ball, at least in my mind!"
Yet the neighbors just think that the weeds are quite kind.

So it struts and it sways in its overgrown space,
An uncelebrated diva in this leafy race.

As dusk settles in, it dons its best light,
With glimmers of humor and giggles at night.
Though never admired, it's quite at its peak,
In the heart of the garden, it's loud but unique.

Memories of the Unseen Flora

In shadows where daisies jump and skip,
A blossom awaits with a comedic quip.
It sways with delight, while the sun shines bright,
Recalling the times when it ruled the night.

Once a grand showgirl with a dazzling hue,
Now it's a wallflower, just passing through.
"I danced with the stars, can't you hear their cheer?"
But only the crickets can lend it an ear.

It whispers to ferns, telling jokes filled with glee,
"What did the tulip say to the bee?"
While the ferns just respond with a rustle and sigh,
"Keep talking to us, we'll take all your lie!"

Yet underneath all the laughter, there's truth in the jive,
In the garden of memories, that's how they thrive.
Though unseen by the world, it'll keep on the show,
With joy and a chuckle, it'll rise up and grow.

A Tale of the Silent Grove

In a grove full of leaves, a story unfolds,
Of a flower so shy, it hardly beholds.
It spreads its soft petals, in secret delight,
With dreams of the day when it shines oh-so-bright.

One day it declared, "I'll throw myself a ball!"
But the critters just giggled, not busy at all.
"You can dance with the shadows, just throw on a glow!"
"But they don't even listen!" the flower did crow.

Around a tree stump, it fashioned a stage,
But weeds stole the limelight, so all was a rage.
With a sigh and a smile, it let out a snort,
"What's wrong with a flower that likes to cavort?"

While no one arrived to join in the blare,
It twirled and spun, enjoying the flair.
In the silence, it found a weird kind of cheer,
A solo performer, its laugh crystal clear.

Fading Color in a Silent World

In a world that's all gray, a splash of surprise,
A blossom pops up with wide-open eyes.
It yells to the daisies, "Come dance in the fog!"
While toads on the sidelines just sit and all hog.

"Look at me go! I'm a rainbow delight!"
The daisies just snicker, "Good luck in the night!"
But our little flower just ignites with pure glee,
"I'll put on a show—won't you come laugh with me?"

As twilight descends, it paints with its heart,
A folly of colors that sets it apart.
Though fading and shy, it sways with a grin,
Creating a riot while trying to win.

"Who needs a crowd when I've got such a soul?"
An actor alone, yet still playing a role.
In whispers it giggles, a comical sight,
In a fading color, that shines through the night.

www.ingramcontent.com/pod-product-compliance
Lightning Source LLC
Chambersburg PA
CBHW070335120526
44590CB00017B/2897